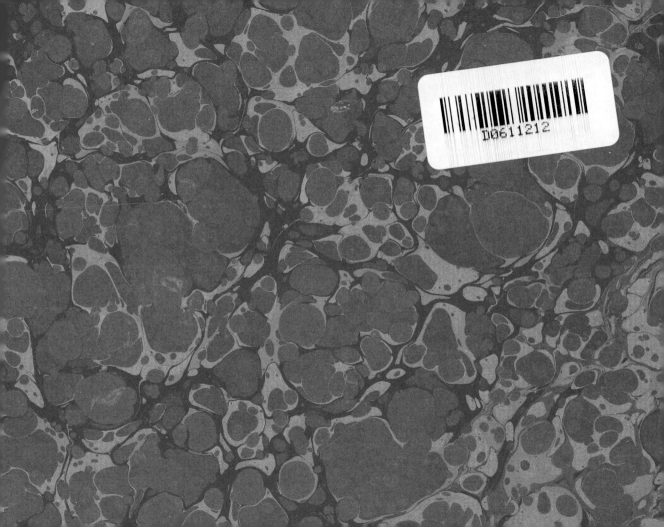

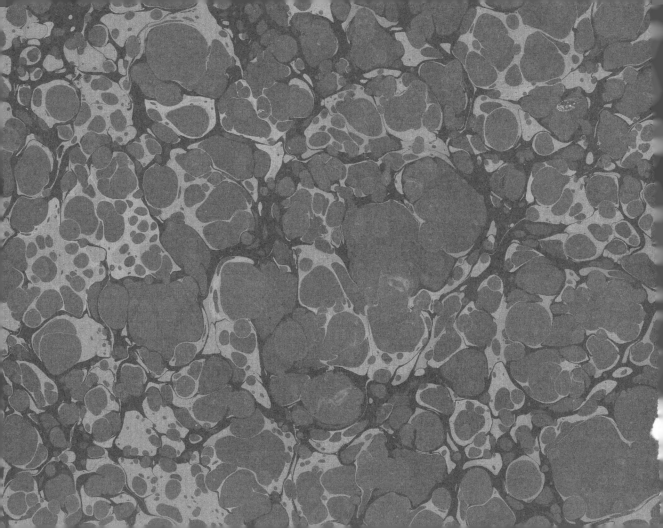

IN TIMES OF

Grief

IN TIMES OF
Grief

CONNIE HARRISON

WITH

EVEY SPENN

QUEST BOOKS
The Theosophical Publishing House

Wheaton, IL U.S.A. / Madras, India / London, England

QUEST BOOKS
The Theosophical Publishing House
P.O. Box 270
Wheaton, IL 60189-0270

A publication of the Theosophical Publishing House,
a department of the Theosophical Society in America

This publication was made possible with the assistance of the Kern Foundation

Design by *The Bridgewater Book Company Ltd / Sarah Bentley*

Library of Congress Cataloging-in-Publication Data
In times of Grief : an inspirational treasury of spiritual texts /
edited by Connie Harrison and Evey Spenn
p.   cm.
ISBN 0-8356-0737-2 : $14.00
1. Consolation. 2. Bereavement--Religious aspects.   I. Spenn,
Evey. II. Harrison, Connie.
BL65.B4715 1995
291.4'3--dc20   94-44556
                                                                    CIP

Printed and bound in Singapore.

*Every effort has been made to find the copyright owner
of the material used. However, there are a few quotations
that have been impossible to trace, and we would be glad to
hear from the copyright owners of these quotations so that
acknowledgment can be made in any future edition.*

DEDICATION

*This book is dedicated to the
memory of Paul and Jackie*

————— •◆• —————

THANKS

*With thanks to Ron Spenn,
Dorothy Johnson, Susan Mears
and Canon Kenneth Parry.*

CONTENTS

Grief

The Loss

New Life

INTRODUCTION

GRIEF is an emotion that we will all experience at some point in our lives. In coming to terms with our own grief, we found that wise and healing thoughts from different ages and spiritual traditions helped us through the grieving process. In this collection, we share our favorites.

Like you, we have suffered the loss of loved ones. The sudden death of Connie's husband Paul of a heart attack and of Evey's twelve-year-old daughter Jackie in a road accident were the most traumatic.

Your experience will be different than ours, yet through this book we can touch each other in a common bond of shared sorrow. Only when our grief has been worked through, can we, like you, move on slowly, but inevitably, to build a new life.

When we have been deeply carved by grief, we are capable of true compassion.

We know that comfort is really beyond words,

yet we would take your hand

and look into your eyes,

THROUGH THE WORDS.

Allow your cleansing tears to flow, for you are being molded and transformed into a being of great beauty.

Daily, we will be sending love and healing to all who have picked up this book. May the Great and Holy Spirit who is in, and yet beyond, all creeds and spiritual paths wonderfully bless and comfort you.

WE LOVE YOU

Connie & Evey

Grief

GRIEF

We must ALLOW *ourselves to* GRIEVE *– To let go of the stiff upper lip.*

Sometimes we feel too dammed up to weep; perhaps that's a time to bash pillows and shout out our grief and anger.

Allow friends to care for and touch you.

A silent hug can be of more comfort than a string of fine words.

Sometimes when we recollect things done, or left undone – said, or left unsaid – we have feelings of guilt.

Be gentle with yourself. For we are only human, as were loved ones we lost. They will totally understand.

FORGIVE THEM. FORGIVE YOURSELF. BE AT PEACE.

LA MUSES DANS LA FORET
Alphonse Osbert
Died 1939

Do not stand at my grave and weep:
    I am not there,
I do not sleep,
I am a thousand winds that blow.
I am the diamond's gilt on snow.
I am the sunlight on ripened grain,
I am the gentle autumn's rain.
When you awaken in the morning's
    hush,
I am the swift uplifting rush
Of quiet birds in circled light.
I am the soft stars that shine at night.
Do not stand at my grave and cry;
I am not there,
I did not die.

ANONYMOUS

In desperate hope I go and search for her in all the corners of
    my room: I find her not.
My house is small and what once has gone from it can never be
    regained.
But infinite is thy mansion, my Lord, and seeking her I have come
    to thy door.
I stand under the golden canopy of thine evening sky and I lift
    my eager eyes to thy face.
I have come to the brink of eternity from which nothing can
    vanish - no hope, no happiness, no vision of a face seen through tears.
Oh, dip my emptied life into that ocean, plunge it into the
    deepest fullness. Let me for once feel that lost sweet touch in
the allness of the universe.

RABINDRANATH TAGORE
Collected Poems and Plays

Impermanent, alas, are all conditioned things,
Their nature is to arise and pass.
They come into existence, then they cease;
Their allaying, their calming, is peace.

Samyutta Nikaya, Vol II

Blessed are they that mourn:
for they shall be comforted.

Authorised Version Bible, Matthew 5, v.4

Grief

DAY-DREAMS ON
THE SEA SHORE
Edith Hume 1862–92

Grief

I am standing on the sea shore. A ship sails and spreads her white sails to the morning breeze and starts for the ocean. She is an object of beauty and I stand watching her till at last she fades on the horizon, & someone at my side says, 'She is gone'. Gone where? Gone from my sight, that is all; she is just as large in the masts, hull and spars as she was when I saw her, and just as able to bear her load of living freight to its destination.

The diminished size and total loss of sight is in me, not in her; and just at the moment when someone at my side says, 'She is gone', there are others who are watching her coming, and other voices take up a glad shout, 'There she comes', and that is Dying.

BISHOP BRENT *Source Unknown*

Death's stamp gives value to the coin of life; making it possible to buy with life what is truly precious.

RABINDRANATH TAGORE
Collected Poems and Plays

Grief should be the Instructor of the wise. Sorrow is Knowledge: they who know the most Must mourn the deepest.

LORD BYRON *Manfred*

Grief

O Jonathan, in your death I am stricken,
  I am desolate for you, Jonathan my brother.
Very dear to me you were,
  your love to me more wonderful
than the love of a woman.

2 Samuel, 1:24–26

o bond
In closer union knits to human hearts
Than fellowship in grief

ROBERT SOUTHEY
ROBERT SOUTHEY
Joan of Arc and Minor Poems

Grief

C an I see another's woe,
  And not be in sorrow too?
Can I see another's grief,
And not seek for kind relief?

WILLIAM BLAKE
Songs of Innocence

E xcept a corn of wheat fall into the ground and die, it abideth alone; but if it die, it bringeth forth much fruit.

Authorised Version Bible, John 12, v.24

Grief

PROCRIS AND CEPHALUS *John Roddam Spencer 1829–1908*

Grief

The Spirit that is in all beings
is immortal in them all:
for the death of what cannot die,
cease thou to sorrow.

The Bhagavad Gita

"Alas, poor world what treasure hast thou lost!"
What face remains alive that's worth the viewing?
Whose tongue is music now? what canst thou boast
Of things long since, or anything ensuing?
The flowers are sweet, their colours fresh and trim;
But true sweet beauty liv'd and died with him.

WILLIAM SHAKESPEARE
Venus and Adonis

They that sow in tears shall reap in joy.

Authorised Version Bible, Psalm 126, v. 5

Grief

A thousand years as a day to you Lord
  A day to me is as a thousand years.
My fairest one you've taken home, and left me
  A pile of books and toys, and nights of tears.

A year to You is as a page in turning
  A year to me, is as a lifetime spent.
In picking up bright threads, and weaving carefully
  A pattern that may last and not be rent.

Oh what is life that we should name it precious?
  And what is death, that we should shun it so?
Bright scented flowers surrounded you, and rightly.
  Their Spirit perfume seemed with you to flow.

Another year has passed, my weavings set now.
  The pattern is not perfect, but it's set.
The longest life is but a season passing,
  So I will dry my tears—but not forget.

EVEY SPENN

Grief

Death is not the extinguishing of
the light, but the putting out of the lamps
because the dawn has come.

RABINDRANATH TAGORE
Collected Poems and Plays

Ye shall be sorrowful,
but your sorrow shall be turned into joy.

Authorised Version Bible, John 16, v. 20

Do not be afraid of death.
We shall go out into
the sunshine to meet our best
dreams and realize them.
Meet death with a smile.
It is truly our friend.
Trust yourself to Life
and to Life on
the other side too.

CLARA CODD
Trust Yourself to Life

iving and dying may be the same thing,
and the fact that we have separated them
may be the source of great sorrow.

KRISHNAMURTI
Commentaries on Living III

O heavenly Love,
how precious still,
In days of weariness and ill,
In nights of pain and helplessness,
To heal, to comfort, and to bless.

HORATIUS BONAR
O Love of God, how strong and true

I sometimes hold it half a sin
To put in words the grief I feel;
For words, like Nature, half reveal
And half conceal the Soul within.

ALFRED, LORD TENNYSON *In Memoriam*

When thou passest through the waters,
I will be with thee; and through the rivers, they shall not overflow thee:
when thou walkest through the fire, thou shalt
not be burned; neither shall the flame kindle upon thee.

Authorised Version Bible, Isaiah 43, v.2

Grief

I WOULD MAINTAIN the sanctity of human joy and human grief. I bow in reverence before the emotions of every melted heart. We have a human right to our sorrow. To blame the deep grief which bereavement awakens, is to censure all strong human attachments. The more intense the delight in their presence, the more poignant the impression of their absence; and you cannot destroy the anguish unless you forbid the joy. A morality which rebukes sorrow rebukes love. When the tears of bereavement have had their natural flow, they lead us again to life and love's generous joy.

JAMES MARTINEAU
Endeavours after the Christian Life: Discourses

Life is eternal; and love is immortal; and death
is only a horizon; and a horizon is nothing save
the limit of our sight.

A Commendatory Prayer ANONYMOUS

Grief

I have seen death too often
to believe in death.
It is not an ending -
but a withdrawal.
As one who finishes
a long journey,
Stills the motor,
Turns off the lights,
Steps from his car,
And walks up the path
To the home that awaits him.

DON BLANDING *'A Journey Ends'*

Grief drives men into the habits of serious
reflection, sharpens the understanding and
softens the heart.

JOHN ADAMS
Letter to Thomas Jefferson, 6 May 1816

⊶⊷ ⊶⊷

Turn thee unto me, and have mercy upon me, for
I am desolate and afflicted.
The troubles of my heart are enlarged: O bring
thou me out of my distresses.

Authorised Version Bible, Psalm 25, v. 16–17

Grief

HEROIC STORIES
Louisa De La Poeur,
Marchioness of Waterford
1818–1891

Grief

But the truth is, death is not the ultimate reality. It looks black, as the sky looks blue; but it does not blacken existence, just as the sky does not leave its stain upon the wings of the bird.

RABINDRANATH TAGORE
Collected Poems and Plays

REMEMBER me
when I am gone away,
Gone far away
into the silent land;
When you can no more
hold me by the hand,
Nor I half turn to go
yet turning stay.
Remember me
when no more day by day
You tell me of our future
that you planned:
Only remember me;
you understand.
It will be late to counsel then
or pray.

Yet if you should forget me
for a while
And afterwards remember,
do not grieve:
For if the darkness
and corruption leave
A vestige of the thoughts
that once I had,
Better by far
you should forget and smile
Than that you should
remember
and be sad.

CHRISTINA ROSSETTI

H o w do I love thee?
Let me count the ways.
I love thee to the depth
and breadth and height
  My soul can reach,
when feeling out of sight
  For the ends of Being
  and ideal Grace.
I love thee to the level
  of every day's
  Most quiet need,
by sun and candlelight.
  I love thee freely
as men strive for Right;

I love thee purely,
  as they turn from Praise.
I love thee
  with the passion put to use
In my old griefs,
  and with my childhood's faith
I love thee with a love
I seemed to lose
With my lost saints, -
I love thee with the breath,
Smiles, tears, of all my life!
- and if God choose,
I shall but love thee
better after death.

ELIZABETH BARRETT BROWNING
Aurora Leigh

*P*eace, peace!
  he is not dead, he doth not sleep - He hath
awakened from the dream of life.

PERCY BYSSHE SHELLEY
The Poetical Works of Percy Bysshe Shelley

THE LOSS

In coming to terms with our loss, we may experience many conflicting emotions, some so strong, or even violent, as to shock us.

Remind yourself that whatever you experience is a necessary part of the healing process. Express in whatever way is natural to you your sorrow, anger, frustration, loneliness, and bewilderment.

BUT – NOW *is the time to accept what can never be changed.*

NOW *is the time to begin exploring the new life that beckons.*

NOW *is the time to remember that deep grief, prolonged, can become pure self pity –*

BE STRONG, BRAVE SOUL.

THE REVELATION
Baron Arild Rosenkrantz
1870–1940

The Loss

AFTER a while you learn
the subtle difference
between holding a hand
and chaining a soul.
And you learn that love
doesn't mean leaning
and company
doesn't mean security.
And you begin to learn
that kisses aren't contracts
and presents aren't promises.
And you begin to accept
your defeats with your head up
and your eyes open
and with the grace of an adult,
not the grief of a child.

AND you learn to build
all your roads on today
because tomorrow's ground
is too uncertain for your plans.

AFTER a while you learn
that even sunshine burns
if you get too much.
So plant your own garden
and decorate your own soul
instead of waiting
for someone to bring you flowers.
And you will learn
that you really can endure –
that you really are strong.
And you really do
have worth.

ANONYMOUS

The Loss

WHEN you are joyous,
look deep into your heart
and you will find
it is only that
which has given you sorrow
that is giving you joy.
When you are sorrowful
look again in your heart
and you shall see
that in truth
you are weeping
for that which has been
your delight.
Some of you say
"Joy is greater than sorrow,"
and others say,

"Nay, sorrow is the greater,"
But I say unto you
they are inseparable.
Together they come,
and when one sits alone
with you at your board,
remember
that the other is asleep
upon your bed.
Verily you are suspended
like scales
between your sorrow
and your joy.
Only when you are empty
are you at a standstill
and balanced.

KAHLIL GIBRAN
The Prophet

God is our refuge and strength,
a very present help in trouble.
Therefore will not we fear –

Authorised Version Bible, Psalm 46, v.1-2

Evening precedes morning,
and night becomes dawn.

IDRIES SHAH
The Way of the Sufi

Let not your heart be troubled:
ye believe in God, believe also in me.
In my Father's house are many mansions:
if it were not so, I would have told you.
I go to prepare a place for you.
And if I go and prepare a place for you,
I will come again, and receive you unto
myself; that where I am, there ye may be
also.

Authorised Version Bible John 14, v. 1–3

The more we know, the more fully we trust,
for we shall feel with utter certainty that
we and our dead are alike in the hands of
perfect Power and perfect Wisdom directed by
perfect Love.

C.W. LEADBEATER
Release into Light

But every morning the day is reborn among the newly-blossomed flowers with the same message retold and the same assurance renewed that death eternally dies, that the waves of turmoil are on the surface, and that the sea of tranquillity is fathomless. The curtain of night is drawn aside and truth emerges without a speck of dust on its garment, without a furrow of age on its lineaments.

RABINDRANATH TAGORE
Sadhana

Better than a thousand useless words is one single word that gives peace.

The Dhammapada

The Loss

 will be glad and rejoice in thy mercy: for thou hast considered my trouble; thou hast known my soul in adversities.

Authorised Version Bible, Psalm 31, v. 7

Not till the loom is silent,
And the shuttles cease to fly
Shall God unroll the pattern
And explain the reason why.

The dark threads are as needful
In the Weaver's skilful hand
As the threads of gold and silver
In the pattern that He has planned.

ANONYMOUS

The Loss

aith is the bird that feels the light
and sings when the dawn is still dark.

RABINDRANATH TAGORE
Collected Poems and Plays

By the Glorious
Morning Light,

And by the Night
When it is still, –

Thy Guardian Lord
Hath not forsaken thee,
Nor is He displeased.

And verily the hereafter
Will be better for thee
Than the present.

The Holy Qur'an

There are only two faces to existence –
birth and death – and life survives them
both, just so sunrise and sunset are not
essentially different: it all depends on
whether one is facing east or west.

JOY MILLS
Release into Light

The Loss

*S*igns from the soul come silently
as silently as the sun enters
the darkened world.

Tibetan Saying

L ift your heart –
for the longest night has already passed.
Walk out with loving eyes,
And search for the first tender shoots.
Brave and foolish they are,
in the frosty air -
Ready to face the chill blast
of winter still to come.
Defiantly Positive
Pointing upwards like small spires
of inspiration.
Think on them, and let your spirit soar.

EVEY SPENN

Abide in me, and I in you.
As the branch cannot bear fruit
of itself, except it abide in
the vine;
no more can ye,
except ye abide in me.

Authorised Version Bible, John 15, v. 4

ix your mind on Me alone, place your intellect
in Me, then you shall, no doubt, live in Me alone.

The Bhagavad Gita

34

The Loss

Much of your pain
is self-chosen.
It is the bitter potion
by which the physician
within you heals your sick self.
Therefore trust the physician,
and drink his remedy
in silence
and tranquillity:
For his hand,
though heavy and hard,
is guided by the tender hand
of the Unseen,
And the cup he brings,
though it burn your lips
has been fashioned
of the clay
which the Potter
has moistened
with His own sacred tears.

KAHLIL GIBRAN
The Prophet

The Loss

ONE NIGHT I had a dream.
I dreamed I was walking along the beach with God and across the sky flashed scenes from my life. For each scene I noticed two sets of footprints in the sand, one belonged to me and the other to God.

When the last scene of my life flashed before us I looked back at the footprints in the sand. I noticed that at times along the path of life there was only one set of footprints.

I also noticed that it happened at the very lowest and saddest times of my life.

This really bothered me and I questioned God about it. "God, You said that once I decided to follow You, You would walk with me all the way but I noticed that during the most troublesome time in my life there is only one set of footprints. I don't understand why in times when I needed You most, You would leave me."

God replied, "My precious, precious child, I love you and I would never, never leave you during your times of trials and suffering.

When you see only one set of footprints it was then that I carried you."

ANONYMOUS

The Loss

From what are pleasure and pain derived?
    What is there to be happy or unhappy about?
When I search for the ultimate nature
    Who is there to crave and what is there
to crave for?

SHANTIDEVA
A Guide to the Bodhisattva's Way of Life

When one sees Eternity in things that pass
away and Infinity in finite things, then
one has pure knowledge.

            The Bhagavad Gita

H ave We not
Expanded thee thy breast? –

And removed from thee
Thy burden

The which did gall
Thy back? –

And raised high the esteem
In which thou art held?

So, verily,
With every difficulty,
There is relief:
Verily, with every difficulty
There is relief.

The Holy Qur'an

S eek an understanding of love
as you would of eternal life.
For if you have love then
you have eternal life.

From the Teachings of 'Zed'

The Loss

Drop Thy still dews of quietness,
    Till all out striving cease;
Take from our souls the strain and stress,
    And let our ordered lives confess
The beauty of Thy peace.

JOHN GREENLEAF WHITTIER
Dear Lord and Father of Mankind
The Methodist Hymn Book

Seek an understanding of love as you would of eternal life.
For if you have love then you have eternal life.

From the Teachings of 'Zed'

YOU know nothing of yourself here
    and in this state.

You are like the wax in the honeycomb:
    what does it know of fire or guttering?
When it gets to the stage of the waxen
    candle and when light is emitted,
then it knows.

    Similarly, you will know that when you
were alive you were dead,
    and only thought yourself alive.

IDRIES SHAH
The Way of the Sufi

The Loss

The voice of Nature loudly cries,
    And many a message from the skies,
That something in us never dies.

ROBERT BURNS
Tam O'Shanter

For, lo, the winter is past,
  the rain is over and gone;
The flowers appear on the earth;
the time of the singing of birds
is come –

Authorised Version Bible,
The Song of Solomon – 2, v. 11–12

Though nothing can bring back the hour
 Of splendour in the grass,
of glory in the flower;
We will grieve not,
rather find Strength
in what remains behind;
In the primal sympathy
Which having been must ever be;
In the soothing thoughts that spring
Out of human suffering;
In the faith that looks through death,
In years that bring the philosophic mind.

WILLIAM WORDSWORTH
Poetical Works

From delusion lead me to Truth.
From darkness lead me to Light.
From death lead me to Immortality.

Brihad-Aranyaka Upanishad

PEACE I leave with you,
    my peace I give unto you:
not as the world giveth,
    give I unto you.
Let not your heart be troubled,
    neither let it be afraid.

Authorised Version Bible, John, v. 14.27

New Life

NEW LIFE

It is time to say "YES" to life; to make friends with the new person that grief has sculpted.

This can become a time of great creativity and renewal, of new ventures, of deep exploration into our most absorbing interest.

Though we may have forced ourselves into a new hobby or a new house, we can with gentleness and grace be open now to the opportunities that life will offer us.

Whatever life brings, we can keep a balance, and –

Follow the Heart as well as the Head.

GOD BLESS YOU

THE HEART OF THE ROSE
Sir Edward Coley Burne-Jones
1833–1898

New Life

They that love beyond the world
cannot be separated by it.
Death cannot kill what never dies -

WILLIAM PENN
Some Fruits of Solitude

That serene and blessed mood,
  In which the affections gently lead us on, -
Until, the breath of this corporeal frame
And even the motion of our human blood
Almost suspended, we are laid asleep
In body, and become a living soul;
While with an eye made quiet by the power
Of harmony, and the deep power of joy,
We see into the life of things.

WILLIAM WORDSWORTH *Poetical Works*

Thus should you think of all this fleeting world;
  A star at dawn, a bubble in a stream;
A flash of lightning in a summer cloud,
  A flickering lamp, a phantom and a dream.

Diamond Sutra

Look to this day!
For it is life,
the very life of life.
In its brief course
lie all the varieties
and realities
of your existence:
the bliss of growth,
the glory of action,
the splendour of beauty.
For yesterday
is already a dream
and tomorrow
is only a vision,
but today, well-lived,
makes every yesterday
a dream of happiness,
and every tomorrow
a vision of hope.
Look well, therefore,
to this day!
Such is the salutation
of the dawn.

Sanskrit

New Life

Look within, and behold how the moonbeams of that Hidden One shine in you.

Poems of Kabir

From the world of the senses,

Arjuna, comes heat and comes cold,

and pleasure and pain.

They come and they go:

they are transient.

Arise above them, strong soul.

The Bhagavad Gita

hy word is a lamp unto my feet and a light unto my path.

Authorised Version Bible, Psalm 119, v. 105

*E*verything is affected by and is part
    of everything else, changing constantly
from one state to another.
    The rain becomes the river;
the river surrenders to the sea
    and the cycle begins over again.
Nothing is ever lost.

    The melody changes –
the dance goes on.

Connie Harrison

New Life

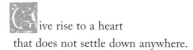
ive rise to a heart
that does not settle down anywhere.

Diamond Sutra

And when the earth shall claim your limbs,
then shall you truly dance.

KAHLIL GIBRAN *The Prophet*

When you grow weary of the boasts of men,
    Go to a tree my friend -
one that has stood
Long patient years within a silent wood.
Beneath its branches you will find again
A thing long lost, trees are content to be
As God created them.
No bough that turns its golden thoughts
to autumn ever yearns
Beyond a hillside's immortality.
Go to a tree in silence, you will find
In the soft eloquence of bud and leaf
Serenity beyond the voice of grief
And faith beyond the reach of humankind.
Man spends his noisy days in search of gain
While trees find God in sunlight, soil and rain.

ANONYMOUS

A RELUCTANT FAREWELL
Jules Gerardet, Born 1856

New Life

My heart today smiles
    at its past night of tears
like a wet tree glistening
    in the sun
after the rain is over.

RABINDRANATH TAGORE
Collected Poems and Plays

Spring will come.
  Come enter
the reasoning of minds
by letting go of mind.
Come turn on the light
of change.
See how the wheel spins.
The hour glass
needs turning again.
The sun reaches its zenith.
The moon waxes and wanes.
Swallows return.
Worms grow old
and lethargic.
Shocking pink babies
replace them.
Come, Rejoice -
Allow the spirit of Spring
to enter your soul.

EVEY SPENN

Be still, and know that
I am God.

Authorised Version Bible, Psalm 46, v. 10

The moon shines in my body, but my

blind eyes cannot see it:

The moon is within me, and so is the sun.

Poems of Kabir

There is a stillness,
    Not immobility
Which moves with movement
    In perfect unity.

There is a silence,
    Of creativity
Which lies concealed
    In life's activity.

There is a peace,
    Not mere passivity
Which is untouched
    By life's duality.

There is a happiness,
    The simplicity
Of being, and accepting
    All as transitory.

CATHERINE HEWITT
Poems by a Lay Buddhist

_BY THY GRACE I remember my Light,
and now gone is my delusion.
My doubts are no more, my faith is firm;
and now I can say

'Thy will be done'.

The Bhagavad Gita

All shall be well,
and all shall be well,
and all manner of thing
shall be well –

JULIAN OF NORWICH
Revelations of Divine Love

New Life

HOPE IN THE PRISON OF DESPAIR
Evelyn de Morgan
1855–1919

New Life

I HAVE seen thee.
In the face of a child,
In the blossoms
on bare branches,
In the moonlight
and the sunset.
I have seen thee.

I have heard thee.
In the song of a bird
In the laughter
of children at play
In the wind
and the rain.
I have heard thee.

I have felt thee.
In the touch of a friend
In the warmth of the sun
upon my face.
In the waters
and the gentle breeze.
I have felt thee.

I have been with thee.
In joy and sadness
In the long and sleepless night
I have felt thy love
and know that all is well.
I have been with thee.

CONNIE HARRISON

New Life

Oh let us live in joy,
　　although having nothing!
In joy let us live like
　　spirits of light!

The Dhammapada

All, everything that I understand,
I understand only because I love.

LEO TOLSTOY *War and Peace*

If I take the wings of the morning,
　　and dwell in the uttermost parts of the sea;
Even there shall thy hand lead me,
and thy right hand shall hold me.
If I say, Surely the darkness shall
cover me; even the night shall be
light about me.
Yea, the darkness hideth not from thee;
but the night shineth as the day:
the darkness and the light,
are both alike to thee.

Authorised Version Bible, Psalm 139, v. 9–12

New Life

I n any way that men love me in that same way they find my love: for many are the paths of men, but they all in the end come to me.

The Upanishads

W hat shall be my legacy?
The blossoms of Spring,
The cuckoo in the hills,
The leaves of Autumn.

Master Ryokan TRANSLATOR UNKNOWN

New Life

For I am persuaded, that neither death, nor life, nor angels, nor principalities, nor powers, northings present, nor things to come, Nor height, nor depth, nor any other creature, shall be able to separate us from the love of God.

Authorised Version Bible, Romans 8, v. 38–39

To every thing
there is a season,
and a time to every purpose
under the heaven:
A time to be born,
and a time to die;
a time to plant,
and a time to pluck up
that which is planted;
A time to weep,
and a time to laugh;
a time to mourn,
and a time to dance.

Authorised Version Bible,
Ecclesiastes 3, v.1,2,4

New Life

And God shall wipe away all tears from their eyes; and there shall be no more death, neither sorrow, nor crying, neither shall there be any more pain: for the former things are passed away.

Authorised Version Bible.
Revelation 21, v. 4

Lo, I am with you always, even unto the end of the world.

Authorised Version Bible.
Matthew 28, v. 20

Let this be my last word that I trust in Thy Love.

RABINDRANATH TAGORE
Collected Poems and Plays

New Life

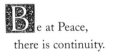

Be at Peace,
there is continuity.

CONNIE HARRISON

ACKNOWLEDGMENTS

THE COMPILERS ACKNOWLEDGE WITH GRATITUDE THE COURTESY OF THE FOLLOWING INDIVIDUALS AND COMPANIES IN PERMITTING THE USE OF COPYRIGHT MATERIAL.

Bhagavad Gita The, translated by Juan Mascaro. Founder Editor (1944-64): E.V. Rieu. Editor: Betty Radice. Penguin Classics 1962. Pages 51. 116. 122. 49 © Juan Mascaro. Reproduced by permission of Penguin Books Ltd.

Bible. Extracts from the Authorised Version of the Bible (the King James Bible), the rights in which are vested in the Crown, are reproduced by permission of the Crown's patentee, Cambridge University Press.

Dhammapada, The, translated by Juan Mascaro. Founder Editor (1944–64): E.V. Rieu. Editor: Betty Radice. Penguin Classics 1973. Pages 50. 64 © Juan Mascaro. Reproduced by permission of Penguin Books Ltd.

Divine Love, Revelations of, Julian of Norwich. Founder editor: E.V. Rieu (1944–64). Editor: Betty Radice. Penguin Classics 1966. Page 35 © Clifton Wolters. Reproduced by permission of Penguin Books Ltd.

Go to a Tree, Anon, reproduced by kind permission of the Men of the Trees (a registered charity), Sandy Lane, Crawley Down, West Sussex, England, RH10 4HS

Lay Buddhist, Poems by a, Hewitt Catherine. By permission of Catherine Hewitt.

Sufi, The Way of the, Shah Idries. Pages 79. 272. First published by Jonathan Cape 1968 © Idries Shah 1968. Reproduced by permission of Jonathon Cape.

Upanishads, The, translated and selected by Juan Mascaro. Founder editor (1944–64): E.V. Rieu. Editors: Betty Radice and Robert Baldick, C.A. Jones (1964–72) Pages 23. 127. Reproduced by permission of Penguin Books Ltd.

Zed, the Teachings of, by permission of Jane Tinworth and David Ferguson.

The Publisher would like to

thank *The Fine Art Picture*

Library for all the pictures used

in this book.

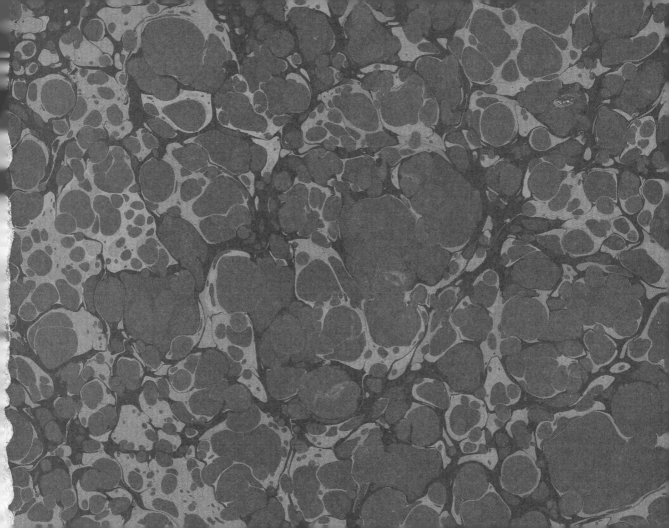

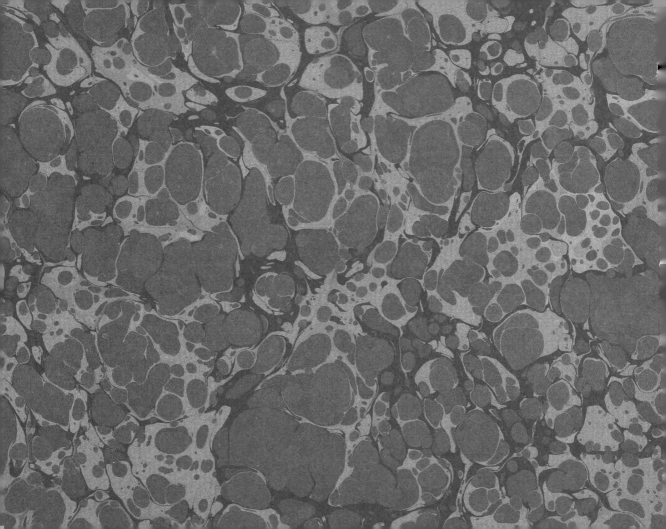